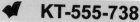

A PARRAGON BOOK

Published by Parragon Book Service Ltd,
Units 13-17, Avonbridge Trading Estate, Atlantic Road,
Avonmouth, Bristol BS11 9QD

Produced by The Templar Company plc,
Pippbrook Mill, London Road, Dorking,
Surrey RH4 1JE

Written by Robert Snedden
Series Editor Robert Snedden
Designed by Mark Summersby
Illustrations by Peter Bull Art Studio

Printed and bound in the UK

ISBN 0 7525 1678 7

FACTFINDERS

INVENTIONS

||| •PARRAGON• |||

TITLES IN THIS SERIES INCLUDE:

ASTRONOMY

CARD GAMES

CLANS & TARTANS

FASTEST CARS

FLAGS OF THE WORLD

HANDGUNS & SMALL ARMS

HISTORIC BRITAIN

HUMAN BODY

INVENTIONS

NATURAL DISASTERS

CONTENTS

INTRODUCTION

Throughout history people have searched for ways to make life easier, to do things more efficiently, to travel further and faster and to change the world in which they live. The story of human civilization is also the story of inventiveness. Invention and discovery are what push us forward – each idea leads to a new idea as succeeding generations of scientists and engineers look for ways to build on the discoveries of their predecessors.

The inventor rarely works alone, conjuring ideas out of thin air. Often there is an obvious need for an invention. In order to produce books in any quantity it was necessary to invent type that could be reused and reordered on a printing press to make many books many times. To pump out the water that flooded deep coal mines it was necessary to develop a powerful engine to do the job. The invention of the printing press had a profound effect. Ideas could be communicated more readily, scientists and engineers could share their findings and learn from the work of others without having to write every copy out painstakingly by hand. The steam-engine that was developed to pump water from the mines was changed, adapted and improved and became the power source of the Industrial Revolution that swept the world, driving manufacturing machinery and the railways.

At other times the inventor or experimenter must seem eccentric or foolish. What must casual observers have thought of Benjamin Franklin flying his kite in a thunderstorm to make discoveries about electricity, or the two brothers, Wilbur and Orville Wright, who put the money they made from making bicycles into developing a new form of transport, the aeroplane? Now we see them as pioneers, taking the first steps on a journey of discovery.

In this book we will take a short look at some of the most important inventions of the last 5000 years or so. Among them are obvious world-changers, such as the wheel, which, in its many forms from the wheels on a chariot to the gear wheels in an engine, has transformed civilization, and the radio, which revolutionized communication. There are also inventions that seem at first to be not so remarkable, yet try to imagine what the world would be like if there were no spectacles to correct eyesight defects and no lightbulbs to provide a ready source of lighting at night.

The world is full of inventions. Everything around you, from the simple paperclip to the powerful computer and the pop-up toaster had to be thought of by someone and developed, perhaps by teams of people, to take the forms we see and take for granted every day. What will be the next world changing invention, and will we recognize it when it first appears? Whatever the answer, humans will continue to invent things – it's in our nature.

THE WHEEL

The invention of the wheel is often described as one of humanity's great leaps forward. The wheel is vital to most societies and it is difficult to imagine how civilization would have developed without it. Many people believe that the wheel was invented only once and then spread to the rest of the world, but there is no proof of this. It may have been discovered many times. Exactly where and when this event took place remains unknown, but it is believed to have happened some time during the 4th millenium BC. The earliest evidence of the wheel has been found in the area between the Tigris and Euphrates rivers in modern Iraq, where the ancient civilization of Sumeria flourished. Archaeologists excavating in the ancient city of Uruk uncovered a clay tablet dating from around 3200 to 3100 BC that contained a pictograph of a wheeled cart. Early wheels were solid and measured around 0.5-1.0 m (1.6-3.2 feet) in diameter. They were formed from three planks of wood clamped by wooden struts and bound with leather held in place by copper nails, the heads of which projected beyond the surface of the wheel to protect the rim. The first wheels and axle formed a single piece and turned together, with the entire assembly connected to the frame with leather thongs. The solidly built early wheels were probably ideal for the rough roads of the time.

A wheel made from a single plank.

A strong, three-plank design.

Sections cut out to lighten the weight.

The spoked wheel, invented about 1400 BC.

THE SAIL

No one will ever be able to say for certain where and when the first sail was invented. It may have happened when someone stood up in a small boat on a windy day and discovered that his boat was being pushed along as the wind filled his cloak. From there it would have been a small step to fix a cloth or animal hide to the ship. From what we know of trading in the ancient world it seems likely that sail-powered ships were in use as early as 3500 BC. The earliest record we have of a sail dates from around 3200 BC and shows a boat on the River Nile. The first sails were flat and stiff but they were soon replaced by a single loose sail held at each corner. By the time of the Roman Empire some 3000 years later there were three-masted sailing ships with triangular sails that jutted away from the mast rather like the rigging on a modern yacht, giving the advantage of being able to sail into the wind rather than simply being blown before it.

An early Egyptian sailing ship.

WRITING

Early drawings dating from 12,000 years ago or earlier, drawn, painted or cut into the surface of rocks, have been found on every continent except Antarctica. These are as much a part of the history of writing as of art because some appear to have been designed more for communication than for pleasure. Prehistoric Egyptian potters and masons used marks to identify their handiwork. In China, Africa and the Americas, knotted cords, notched sticks and other devices were used to help with counting or to keep track of time or distance.

A writing system is a collection of arbitrary signs that, in different

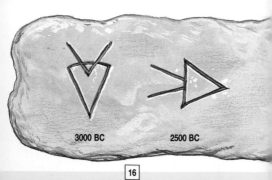

3000 BC   2500 BC

combinations, can represent all the words of a given language. Full writing systems have only emerged during the past 5,000 years. Without a system of writing, few of the technological advances that have taken place would have been possible. Writing allows the creation of a permanent fund of knowledge that succeeding generations can draw on and learn from. Before writing, the only way to pass on experience was by word of mouth. Writing allows complex ideas to be transmitted from place to place. A message that can be written down can be carried any distance and does not depend on the messenger recalling it correctly.

Examples of writing from ancient Mesopotamia showing how the symbol for ox changed over time.

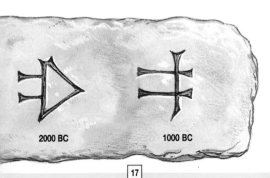

2000 BC   1000 BC

MONEY

No one knows when some form of money was first used as a medium of exchange. In early societies people would directly barter, or exchange, goods and services. The trouble with direct barter is that you have to locate someone who wants the particular thing you can provide and, at the same time, happens to have available for exchange the thing you want. Using money makes the process much easier. All you have to do is find a person who wants what you are selling, get money in exchange for it, and then find another person who has what you want to buy and give him the money for it.

Whatever is chosen for exchange the important

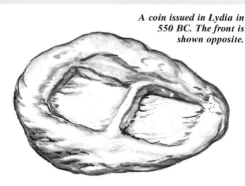

A coin issued in Lydia in 550 BC. The front is shown opposite.

thing is that all parties recognize it as having value. As societies and economies developed, money was used more and more for ordinary trade. In ancient Europe valuable items such as iron arrowheads were exchanged for goods. In Africa and Oceania rare shells or feathers might be used. In Egypt, around 1500 BC, gold ingots were weighed and stamped to show their maximum exchange value. Ancient Babylon had a highly developed monetary system with banks and credit, as did ancient Greece and Rome. Coinage was probably invented in ancient China and reinvented (c.700 BC) by the Lydians (shown here) in what is now Turkey. Paper currency was invented in China, around the 9th century.

PAPER

Paper is made from inter-laced fibres, usually from plants, but sometimes from cloth rags or other materials. It is formed by pulping the fibres and pressing them flat to form a solid surface. The invention of paper is generally credited to Ts'ai Lun, a Chinese court official, in about AD 105. The Chinese had probably made paper from hemp fibres, perhaps as much as 250 years earlier, but it was thick and uneven and was probably used for packing rather than writing on. The oldest known piece of paper used for writing dates from AD 110. Ts'ai Lun was the first to succeed in making paper from vegetable fibres, using mulberry tree bark, rags and old fishing nets, all of which were

soaked, crushed and pressed. The art of paper making was kept secret for 500 years but it eventually spread throughout the world. The Japanese acquired it in the 7th century and in 770 produced the first mass publication, a block-printed Buddhist prayer paper, of which 1,000,000 were printed. In AD 751 the Arab city of Samarkand was attacked by the Chinese. Among the Chinese prisoners taken during the attack were several skilled in the art of papermaking. They were forced by the city's governor to build and operate a paper mill. From here papermaking spread to other Arab cities and then to the West. There were paper mills all over Europe by the 14th century.

A tray with a bamboo grid is lowered into a vat of pulp.

Water is squeezed out of the pulp.

The paper sheet is removed from the mesh and left to dry.

THE COMPASS

The inventor of the magnetic compass is unknown, but there is evidence to suggest that the Chinese were aware that a lodestone, influenced by the Earth's magnetism, could be used to indicate horizontal directions. A Chinese book dating from AD83 describes a device in which a spoon made of magnetized iron ore was placed on a polished bronze plate to see which direction the handle would point in. Even earlier than this is a fourth-century BC reference to people who used a 'south-pointer' so as not to lose their way. It seems likely, however, that the lodestone was first used to determine which way a house should face so as to bring most luck,

rather than acting as a navigational device.

Chinese seamen of the 12th century were probably the first to use a magnetic compass to navigate at sea. By this

time the compass had taken the form of a magnetized needle floating in a container of water. By the end of the 12th century, no one is sure by what route, compasses were being used on European ships as well. By the 13th century the compass card, showing the different points of the compass, had been invented by Petrus Peregrinus, a French scholar. This was placed at the bottom of the box containing the needle so that directions could be read off it easily.

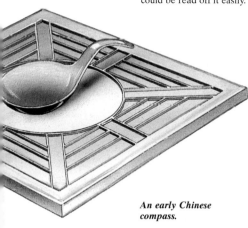

An early Chinese compass.

THE WINDMILL

Windmills are devices that use the energy of the wind to generate power and perform work, such as pumping water or grinding grain. They usually have two or more blades or sails mounted on a shaft, from which the power is taken. The earliest known windmills were built in Persia (now Iran) in about the 7th century AD and were used for pumping water for irrigation and for grinding grain. By the 12th century their use had spread throughout Europe. Early European windmills pumped water or turned the grindstones of corn mills. In Holland they were used to drain the land after the dykes were built. The Dutch mills, as well as smaller mills, had wooden frames with canvas stretched over them to form the sails that turned in the wind.

During the late 19th century thousands of windmills were in use in Europe and in the rural United States, mostly for irrigation. They were gradually replaced by other power sources, such as steam engines running on coal and by electric motors. In recent years there has been a revival of interest in using machines to harness the energy of the wind with many countries investing in wind-energy programs. 'Wind farms' of more than 100 wind turbines can generate hundreds of megawatts of electric power.

A traditional windmill of the type used in the Middle East.

THE MECHANICAL CLOCK

Probably people first began to measure time around 10,000 years ago when agriculture was developed and farmers had to determine the best times to plant. The first people to develop a means of telling time with clocks were the Egyptians. Around 2100 BC they made the first sundials, or shadow clocks, to measure time during the day. At night they observed the positions of the stars, or used slowly burning ropes or candles. By 1500 BC they had invented the water clock, or clepsydra, which used dripping water to power a mechanical device indicating the hour. The water clock remained the best way of telling the time until the advent of mechanical clocks nearly 3,000 years later.

Modern mechanical clocks date from the late Middle Ages. A weight or spring was used to turn a wheel and a system of gears that moved the hands of the clock. A mechanism called an escapement allowed the teeth of one of the gears to 'escape' one by one. Accuracy was considerably improved when the Dutch scientist Christiaan Huygens introduced the pendulum, which regulated the rate at which the escapement moved the gear wheels tooth by tooth, while the escapement kept the pendulum moving.

The earliest mechanical clock, built in China around AD720, was water-powered. Massive gears moved models of the Moon and Sun on a sphere.

SPECTACLES

Around 1286 in Florence, Italy, Alessandro della Spina, making use of the invention of his friend Salvino degli Armati, is credited as having produced the first eye-glasses or spectacles. These had convex lenses, which curve or bulge outwards, and were used for correcting long-sightedness. By the middle of the 14th century spectacles had become fairly common in Europe and can be seen being worn in portrait paintings of the time. It was not until the middle of the 15th century that concave lenses, which curve inwards, for correcting short-sightedness began to appear. These were first made by Nicholas Krebs in Germany.

In 1784 Benjamin Franklin, in the United States, invented bifocal spectacles by mounting concave and convex half lenses for correcting near and long sight in the same frames.

The fact that spectacles did not appear in earlier centuries may in part be attributed to the fact that early glass was rarely totally transparent because of impurities in the ingredients used in its manufacture. Crude lenses have been found dating back to around 2000 BC in Crete and Western Asia, but these may have been used as simple magnifying glasses or for starting fires. Very little was known of optics, the study of light and vision, at the time and there would have been great difficulties in cutting and polishing lenses to give the correct degree of adjustment to the visual defect.

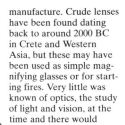

The Emperor Nero is said to have used a monocle made of emerald to improve his vision at the arena. Obviously, this expensive solution would not have been available to everyone!

Spectacles with glass lenses began to appear in the Middle Ages.

MOVABLE TYPE

Johann Gutenberg (c.1398–1468), a German goldsmith, is credited with the invention of printing from movable type. He first experimented with printing about 1440 and by 1450 his invention was ready to be used commercially. Gutenberg introduced a method of casting type in order to produce the large numbers of individual pieces needed to set a whole book. Single letters were engraved in relief and then punched into slabs of brass to produce matrices from which replicas could be cast in molten metal. The characters were combined in a composing stick and then transferred to a frame that held the complete page. Gutenberg also developed an ink that would stick evenly to his metal type. His printing press was an adapted wine press. Gutenberg got into debt and abandoned printing altogether after 1465, possibly because of blindness. Only one major work can definitely be attributed to his workshop – the Gutenberg Bible, set and printed about 1455.

A press of the type used in Gutenberg's time.

THE MICROSCOPE

Magnification using simple lenses was discovered in ancient times, but the development of the modern microscope dates from the construction of compound-lens systems, some time between 1590 and 1610. The credit probably belongs to father and son Dutch lensmakers Hans and Zacharias Jannsen who, in about 1600, constructed a simple instrument that consisted of a pair of lenses mounted in a sliding tube. A compound-lens system using a convex lens in the eyepiece was described by Johannes Kepler in 1611, probably based on work carried out by the Janssens. Improvements to the microscope included the addition of a condenser lens to concentrate light on specimens, a specimen stage to hold the object being examined and gears to control the adjustment of the tube. By the 1680s microscopists had discovered cells, capillaries, blood corpuscles, protozoans

One of van Leeuwenhoek's microscopes.

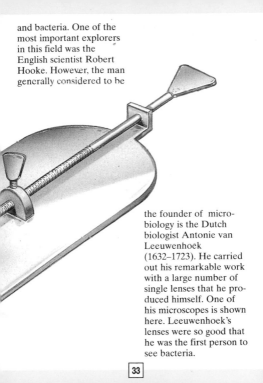

and bacteria. One of the most important explorers in this field was the English scientist Robert Hooke. However, the man generally considered to be the founder of micro-biology is the Dutch biologist Antonie van Leeuwenhoek (1632–1723). He carried out his remarkable work with a large number of single lenses that he produced himself. One of his microscopes is shown here. Leeuwenhoek's lenses were so good that he was the first person to see bacteria.

THE THERMOMETER

Several inventors explored the idea of using the way air expands and contracts as it is heated and cooled as a means of measuring temperature. Around 1603, the great Italian scientist Galileo Galilei (1564–1642) made a device called a thermoscope that consisted of a small glass flask the size of a hen's egg with a slender neck about 36cm (16 in) long. The open end of the neck was placed in a little water which rose and fell in the neck according to the temperature of the air in the flask. The thermoscope was developed by various people, including Galileo's colleague Santorio Santorio and by Galileo himself, to include a numerical scale. In 1641 the Grand Duke of Tuscany invented a thermometer that measured the expansion and contraction of a liquid in the tube. Mercury thermometers were first used in the 1650s. In the early 18th century temperature scales based on agreed reference points (for example, the temperature of a mixture of ice and salt, the boiling point of water, and so forth) were developed by Daniel Gabriel Fahrenheit (1686–1736) and Anders Celsius (1701–1744). These scales are still in use, and the Celsius system (extended in the 19th century) has become the standard scientific temperature scale.

A 17th-century glass thermometer.

34

THE SUBMARINE

The first craft known to have manoeuvred underwater was constructed by Cornelius Drebbel, court engineer to James I of England, and was demonstrated on the River Thames in 1620. Drebbel's craft was propelled by 12 oarsmen, their oars sealed at the locks by leather seals. It apparently submerged by letting water into the hull and surfaced by pumping it back out again. Several inventors were intrigued by the idea of developing an underwater craft but were hampered by the the lack of a reliable power source to propel the vessel. The one-man wooden *Turtle* (shown here), designed by the American David Bushnell in 1775, was driven by hand- and foot-cranked propellers. It towed an explosive charge that, in theory, could be fastened to an enemy ship's hull. The *Turtle's* one foray, against a British ship lying off New York Harbor in 1776, was frustrated because the craft proved difficult to manoeuvre underwater. In 1801, Robert Fulton demonstrated his three-man metal submarine, the *Nautilus*, for the French navy. The *Nautilus*, like the *Turtle*, was driven by a hand-cranked propeller, but a gearing system improved matters. For depth control it had movable horizontal surfaces – the diving planes now used on all modern submarines. Its armament was a towed contact mine, designed to explode when dragged against the enemy target.

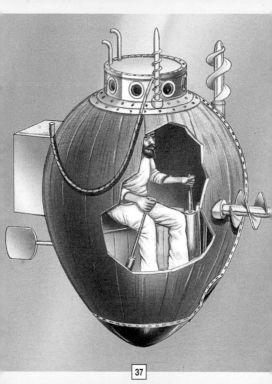

THE CALCULATOR

The Chinese abacus, invented around the 9th century BC was probably the first adding machine. The beads on the wires of the abacus represented numbers and the operator performed calculations by moving the beads around. The earliest-known machine that added numbers without requiring the operator to know how to add was described by Hero of Alexandria in a work dating from around the 2nd century AD. It used gear wheels meshed to form a train of gears and could add up the stades (a measure of distance) that a carriage travelled. The principle on which it operated, based on the rotation of a pegged wheel, is still used in gas meters and car odometers. In the 17th century the French mathematician Blaise Pascal (1623-62) invented an adding machine based on this principle, apparently to help his father, who was a tax official. In the same century the German mathematician Gottfried von Leibniz (1646–1716) produced a multiplying and dividing

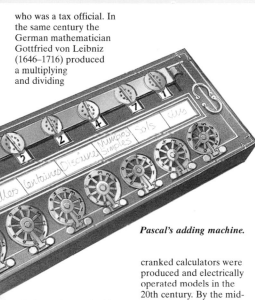

Pascal's adding machine.

calculator that worked by successive adding and subtracting. During the 18th and 19th centuries hand-cranked calculators were produced and electrically operated models in the 20th century. By the middle of the 20th century, the computer began to replace the adding machine.

ELECTRICITY

As early as 600 BC the Greeks were aware of the peculiar properties of amber, a yellow substance made of fossilized resin. When it is rubbed with a piece of fur or cloth, amber will attract small pieces of material such as feathers. Two thousand years later, in the 16th century, William Gilbert, court physician to Queen Elizabeth I, proved that many other substances are also 'electric'. Intrigued by Gilbert's ideas, Otto von Guericke in Germany made a device in 1665 that could generate sizable sparks of what came to be known as static electricity. In 1747, Benjamin Franklin in America and William Watson in England independently concluded that all materials possess an electrical 'fluid' and that the action of rubbing transferred electric fluid from one body to another, electrifying both. Franklin defined the presence of electric fluid as positive and the lack of fluid as negative. In 1752 he carried out his famous kite experiment, in which he flew a kite with a silk thread with a key on the end during a thunderstorm. He was able to charge a device for storing electricity with the key, thus establishing that the static electricity produced in the laboratory and lightning were the same phenomenon on a vastly different scale. Today we know that the phenomenon of electricity involves the movement of tiny subatomic particles called electrons, named after the Greek for amber.

THE STEAM ENGINE

The beginnings of steam power came with the invention in 1698 of Thomas Savery's 'Miner's Friend'. High-pressure steam was injected into a metal chamber then condensed using cold water, the resulting vacuum being used to draw water out of a flooded mine. The first true steam engine was invented about 1712 by another Englishman, Thomas Newcomen. His 'atmospheric engine' used low-pressure steam to displace the air from a cylinder and the vacuum caused a piston to move downward. The Newcomen engine acted only in one direction, and the piston had to be raised by counterweights. Several key improvements were made to the steam engine by James Watt in the 1760s and '70s. He greatly increased the efficiency of the Newcomen engine by keeping the main engine cylinder hot and shunting the cooler, condensing steam to a separate chamber. Watt also devised the first double-acting engine, which powered both the upstroke and the down. This made it possible to attach the piston rod to a crank or set of gears and thus to produce rotary motion to drive the wheels of a carriage or the paddles of a riverboat. Early in the 19th century Richard Trevithick's high-pressure steam engine became the basis for the railway locomotives and river- and ocean-going vessels that revolutionized transport in the 19th century.

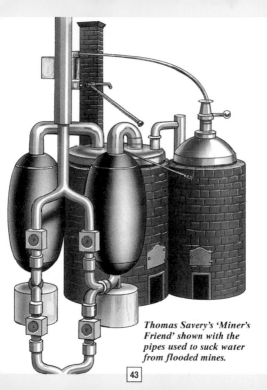

Thomas Savery's 'Miner's Friend' shown with the pipes used to suck water from flooded mines.

THE TELEGRAPH

Around 300 BC the Greeks devised a method of signalling using large vases in a grid of rows and columns that was visible from a distance. Letters were signified according to the positions of vases in the grid. In 1791 Claude Chappe invented optical telegraphy. (Chappe also invented the word telegraph, taken from two Greek words meaning 'far' and 'writing'.) A system of towers were built on hills, each tower being topped by a vertical pole to which was fixed a pivoted arm with a smaller movable arm. These could be put into a variety of positions, rather like a man signalling with flags. Chappe devised a system of 49 different positions for the arms. A network of 120 towers erected between Paris and Toulon allowed a message to be sent 100 times faster than the swiftest courier could achieve. The idea of electric telegraphy came when experimenters noticed that electric charges could be transmitted through wires. In 1836 Charles Wheatstone devised a telegraph based on Hans Christian Oersted's discovery in 1819 that an electric current in a wire would deflect a magnetized needle next to the wire. The five-needle telegraph, patented by Wheatstone and William Fothergill Cooke in London in 1837, had a panel printed with letters and numbers to which the five needles pointed. It was widely used in Britain for sending signals to railwaymen.

THE BICYCLE

The first step toward the development of the bicycle was the invention of the celerifere, or wooden horse, probably in France in the 1790s. The celerifere was propelled by pushing the feet along the ground, had a fixed front wheel and couldn't be steered. In 1817 Karl von Drais invented the draisienne, or dandy horse, which had a steerable front wheel. The first machine with pedals was made in 1839, by Kirkpatrick Macmillan, a Scottish blacksmith. These were connected to the rear wheel by means of cranks.

The French velocipede, invented in the 1860s, had a pedal-driven front wheel that revolved once with each turn of the pedals. The speed of the machine

depended on the size of the front wheel. The front wheel of the penny-farthing, introduced in the 1870s, could be 1.5 m (5 ft) or more, while the back wheel was only one-quarter that size.

In 1879 H.J. Lawson introduced the safety bicycle, with a chain and sprocket driving the rear wheel and in 1885 J.K. Stanley's model, with wheels of equal size, became the basic model for the modern bicycle. Pneumatic tyres were introduced in the 1880s and two- and three-speed gears appeared in the 1890s.

THE HOT-AIR BALLOON

In 1782 the Montgolfier brothers, Joseph Michel and Jacques Etienne, observed that smoke from a fire made a silk bag rise up into the air. On 5 June 1783 they gave a public demonstration of their discovery in the town of Annonay. Their balloon stayed in the air for about 10 minutes, travelling more than 1.6km (about 1 mile) at an altitude of about 1830m (6000 ft). On 19 September the brothers put a sheep, duck and rooster aboard the balloon to see what effect altitude might have on living creatures. On 15 October François Pilâtre de Rozier became the first human to ascend in a balloon. On that occasion the balloon was kept tethered, but on 21 November de Rozier and the Marquis d'Arlandes made the first balloon trip, travelling across the city of Paris. Earlier that year, on 27 August, French chemist J.A.C. Charles had inflated a balloon with hydrogen and launched it from Paris. In December 1783 he and an assistant made the first manned flight in a hydrogen balloon, from Paris to the village of Nesle, 104 km (65 miles) to the north. Hydrogen, and later helium, was found to be superior to hot air for filling a balloon because it is inherently lighter than air and does not need to be heated to produce lift.

THE BATTERY

Around 1780, the Italian scientist Luigi Galvani (1737–98) found that a dissected frog's leg twitched when brought into contact with two different metals, such as brass and iron. Galvani believed that the frog muscle was producing what he called animal electricity. Galvani reported his discovery to another Italian scientist, Alessandro Volta (1745–1827), who repeated the experiments and decided that Galvani's explanation was wrong. He established that a chemical reaction between the brass and iron, separated by the moist tissue of the frog, was generating the electricity, and the frog's leg was simply acting as a detector. In 1800, Volta built a device (shown here) that amplifed the effect. It was made up of stacks of alternating plates of copper, zinc and moistened pasteboard. When the ends were connected up, the voltaic pile as it was called, produced a steady flow of electricity. Volta had invented the battery. This reliable source of electricity was soon being used in laboratories around the world.

The battery, or dry cell, that we use in radios and other portable gadgets today was invented in 1865 by the Frenchman Georges Leclanché. The first rechargeable battery, similar in design to the batteries used in cars today, was invented by another Frenchman, Gaston Planté, in 1859.

THE STEAM LOCOMOTIVE

In 1804 Richard Trevithick became the first person to run a steam engine on rails. He carried out his demonstration at an ironworks in Wales, successfully hauling 10 tons of iron and 70 cheering miners behind his engine. This first rail journey was one way only, when the engine reached the mine it stayed there to power machinery.

In 1808, Trevithick arranged another demonstration, this time in London, when he charged people to see his latest locomotive go round a circular track at 16km/h (10mph).

The first real rail transport link, the Stockton and Darlington Railway was opened in 1825. It was 42km (26 miles) long and was designed to carry coal and passengers. The man behind it was the engineer George Stephenson, who built his first engine in 1814. His engine, the *Locomotion,* was used on the Stockton–Darlington line.

In 1829 a competition was held at Rainhill, between Warrington and Liverpool, to determine which design of locomotive would be best for use on the railways that were planned. It was won by Stephenson's *Rocket*, which had a boiler that was more efficient by far than any produced previously. Eight Rocket-type locomotives were ordered for the new Liverpool and Manchester Railway and the age of the train had begun.

Trevithick's first locomotive was powered by a high-pressure engine.

THE ELECTRIC MOTOR

In 1820 Danish scientist Hans Christian Oersted made an important discovery. He noticed that the needle on a compass moved when it was brought near a wire carrying an electric current. For a long time scientists had suspected that there was a connection between electricity and magnetism. Oersted's discovery led Michael Faraday to make further experiments. In 1821 he found that the force acting between the magnet and the current running through the wire made the magnet move in

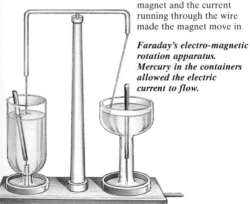

Faraday's electro-magnetic rotation apparatus. Mercury in the containers allowed the electric current to flow.

a circle around the wire. Faraday set up a device that allowed either the magnets or the wires to rotate freely. He called it an electro-magnetic rotation apparatus. When a current was passed through the freely-moving wire it would rotate about the magnet and a freely-moving magnet would rotate about a fixed wire. Faraday had turned electrical energy into mechanical energy. This was the first step towards the electric motor.

In 1830 Joseph Henry made use of electromagnets to construct the first motor that could be used to do work. Within a decade drills and lathes were being powered by electric motors.

A simple electric motor.

Current flows through a coil of wire and the magnetic force makes it rotate.

Battery

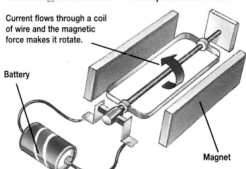

Magnet

PHOTOGRAPHY

Since the 16th century artists and scientists had made use of the fact that light passing through a small hole in one wall of a dark room, a camera obscura, projects an inverted image on the opposite wall. The next stage was to replace the hole with a lens that would make the image brighter and sharper. By the 18th century the room itself had been replaced by a portable box, which artists could use as a sketching aid. In 1725, Johann Heinrich Schulze discovered that certain chemicals, especially silver halides, turn dark when exposed to light. The first successful attempt at capturing a camera obscura image was made by Joseph Nicephore Niepce, who took the first photo-graph, of a view from his window, in 1827. However, Niepce's technique required exposures of several hours and the images were poor. Louis Daguerre, who worked with Niepce,

An early camera made around 1850.

came up with an improved method of creating pictures on silver-coated metal plates, using silver iodide as a light-sensitive coating and developing the image with mercury vapour. This invention, bought by the French government and made public on 19 August 1839, was called the daguerreotype. In 1840, William Henry Talbot in England, invented the calotype, which produced a negative picture on paper. A positive image was made on another sheet of chemically treated paper. Because any number of positives could be made from a single negative, Talbot's invention gained favour.

COMPUTER

English mathematician Charles Babbage first proposed the idea of the computer in 1832. His analytical engine (opposite) had many features of a modern computer, including: input devices, a memory, a computing unit and output devices. Had it ever been built the engine would have had more than 50,000 moving parts. Babbage planned to use perforated cards to program the analytical engine – a method that was used to control automatic silk-weaving machines called Jacquard looms. In 1889 Herman Hollerith, an American inventor, patented a calculating machine that was used to sort information gathered for the 1890 United States census. It also used punched cards. Holes on the cards represented age, income and so on and when one or more metal pins in the machine went through a hole in the card an electric circuit was completed and the total for that category went up. In 1896 Hollerith founded the Tabulating Machine Company, which, in 1924, became International Business Machines Corporation (IBM). In 1939 American physicists John V. Atanasoff and Clifford Berry produced a computer using the binary numbering system. Because binary uses just two digits, 1 and 0, it can easily be represented by electrical circuits, which are either on or off.

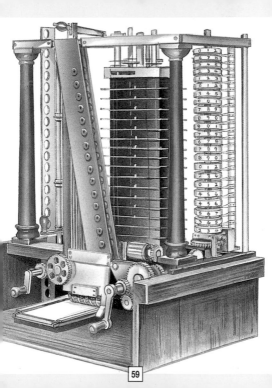

REVOLVER

The term revolver is usually used to mean a repeating pistol that holds its ammunition in a revolving cylinder rather than a magazine. Handguns working on the revolver principle first appeared in 16th-century Europe. The difficulty with early models was igniting the propellant. Matchlock or flintlock

devices did not work well and it was not until the invention of the copper percussion cap in 1815 that a reliable revolver could be developed. An

A Colt revolver.

early form of revolving repeating pistol was the 'pepperbox', which was reminiscent of the early machine-gun, with each cylinder of the revolving cartridge chamber attached to its own barrel.

barrelled revolvers, which were lighter and easier to aim, began to replace the clumsy pepperboxes.

In 1836, the American inventor Samuel Colt began manufacturing a

The pepperbox (so-called because its cluster of barrels resembled a pepper shaker) had the unfortunate tendency of exploding because when one cartridge was fired, it sometimes set off the rest. In addition it was heavy and awkward and, because the barrels were smoothbore, their accuracy was poor. After the 1840s, single-

simple cocking mechanism that has formed the basis of almost every modern revolver. As the hammer cocking the trigger was pulled back, the cylinder rotated and locked in position. The Colt's light trigger pull was popular because it permitted accurate shooting, and rapid fire could be accomplished by 'fanning' (holding the trigger back while slapping the hammer).

MORSE CODE

Wiliam Sturgeon's invention of the electromagnet in 1825 provided a way to transmit and receive electric signals. In partnership with Alfred Vail, Samuel Morse developed a simple operator key, which when depressed completed an electric circuit and sent an electric pulse to a distant receiver. An electromagnet in the receiver was energized by the pulse of current and attracted a soft iron arm, deflecting a line being drawn by a pencil attached to the arm. Morse and Vail, adapted this receiver to print the

A ·—   D —··   G ——·   J ·———
B —···   E ·   H ····   K —·—
C —·—·   F ··—·   I ··   L ·—··

dot and dash symbols of Morse Code, which Morse invented to represent letters and numbers. The two symbols corresponded to long and short pulses. In 1844, Morse gave a successful demonstration of his magnetic telegraph, sending the message 'What hath God wrought' from Baltimore to Washington. Around 1856 he developed a sounding key. Operators learned to decode the sounds and write down the message. Morse's receiver was widely adopted and telegraphs spread across Europe and the USA.

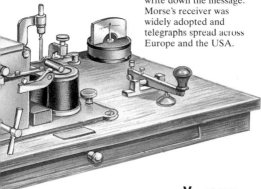

M ——   P ·——·   S ···   V ···—
N —·   Q ——·—   T —   W ·——
O ———   R ·—·   U ··—   X —··—
    Y —·——
    Z ——··

THE ELEVATOR

Steam-powered elevators were used to transport freight in factories and ore in mines in the early 19th century, but they lacked a safety device to stop the elevator if its hoisting mechanism failed or if its supporting cable broke. In 1852, Elisha Graves Otis designed the first safety device for elevators. A series of ratchets were installed down the sides of the upright girders in the lift shaft. If the elevator cable broke a spring-activated stay sprang out to engage the ratchets, halting the elevator. In 1857, Otis installed his first safety-equipped passenger elevator in a five-storey china and glassware store in New York City. Otis's elevators were steam-powered, the elevator car being moved by a system that used a belt-driven winding drum.

The invention of the electric motor made elevators, and therefore skyscrapers, practical. The first electrically driven elevators were installed at the observation tower of the Mannheim Industrial Exhibition of 1880 in Germany. They ascended to a height of 22 metres (72 feet) in 11 seconds (120 metres per minute). Modern high-speed elevators for tall residential or office buildings range in maximum speed from 140 to 550m (460 to 1800 ft) per minute, the fastest elevators obviously being used in the tallest buildings.

The Otis safety elevator.

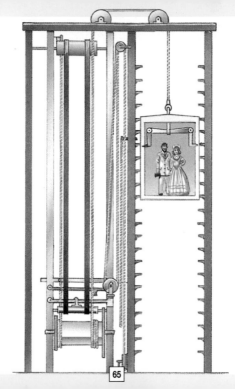

THE LIGHT BULB

During the 1840s many scientists and inventors were trying to develop a workable incandescent electric lamp. One of these experiments involved heating strips of carbon or high-resistance metals to a glowing white-hot temperature by passing an electric current through them, but the heated material soon burned away. In 1878, Sir Joseph Swan (1828–1914) in Britain and Thomas Alva Edison (1847–1931) in America, working independently, developed a successful carbon filament lamp. In 1865 a new and efficient pump had been invented that allowed the air to be pumped out of a vessel, creating a partial vacuum. When an electric current was passed through thin filaments of carbonized threads tightly sealed inside a glass bulb from which the air had been removed the threads did not burn. The voltage was steadily increased until the white heat reached a stable, bright glow. Edison managed to keep his bulbs glowing for 40 hours. Carbon filament lamps were so shock resistant that for many years they were used on board battleships.

Edison also invented the first efficient electricity generators to provide a regular supply of current for his lamps. In 1882 his Pearl Street plant began serving 59 customers in the Wall Street district of Manhattan, supplying electric current for more than a thousand lamps.

THE MOTOR CAR

The first mechanically-powered road vehicle was invented by Nicholas Cugnot of France in 1769. It was a three-wheeled steam carriage made to pull cannons and travelled at a sedate 5km/h (3 mph).

In 1886 two men who were to become famous in car manufacturing were working on petrol-powered cars. On 3 July Karl Benz of Mannheim, Germany, demonstrated his three-wheeled petrol-driven Motorwagen. Just one month later Gottleib Daimler produced his four-wheel model in Cannstadt, 96km (60 miles) away. Both cars travelled at around 16km/h (10 mph). Benz also produced a four-wheeled car in 1893.

By the end of the 19th century several hundred people had bought motor cars. In 1913 Henry Ford opened the first modern car assembly line and began to produce his Model T car in great numbers. This was a car that was made as simply as possible and that many could afford to buy. By 1927 15 million Model T Fords had rolled off the assembly lines of Ford's factories.

Karl Benz's Motorwagen of 1886. Its first trip covered just 800 metres (half a mile).

MOVING PICTURES

Between 1872 and 1877 Eadward Muybridge made a series of photographs using still cameras to make exposures in sequence. He then mounted these on a disk and projected them with a magic lantern to give an illusion of motion. Thomas Alva Edison heard Muybridge give a lecture and started a series of experiments in 1888, beginning with an attempt to record photographs on wax cylinders similar to those used to make the original phonograph recordings. His associate W.K.L. Dickson made a major breakthrough when he used the celluloid film invented by George Eastman instead. Celluloid could be manufactured in long rolls, making it an excellent medium for motion photography, which took up great lengths of film. Between 1891 and 1895, Dickson shot many 15-second films using the Edison camera, or Kinetograph. Feeling that motion pictures would have little public appeal Edison marketed an electrically driven viewing machine, the Kinetoscope, that displayed moving pictures to one viewer at a time. Edison failed to take out patent rights in Europe and Louis and Auguste Lumiere, manufactured a projector based on Edison's device. The birth of the cinema came on 28 December 1895, when the Lumieres presented a programme of motion pictures to a paying audience in the basement of a Paris cafe.

The Kinetoscope.

THE RADIO

The principles of radio were demonstrated in the early 1800s by scientists such as Michael Faraday and Joseph Henry who showed that an electric current flowing in one wire could induce (produce) a current in another wire that was not physically connected to the first. In 1864, James Clerk Maxwell reasoned that an electrical disturbance should travel through space at the speed of light. In the late 1880s Heinrich Hertz produced electromagnetic waves using oscillating circuits to transmit and receive radio waves. Seemingly it did not occur to Hertz to use electromagnetic waves for long-distance communication. It was left to Guglielmo Marconi to produce the first practical wireless telegraph system in 1895. In 1896 he received the first wireless patent from the British government and in March 1899 he sent the first wireless telegraph message across the English Channel. In a short time wireless sets were installed in lighthouses along the English coast, permitting communication with radios aboard nearby ships and the use of radio for emergencies at sea was soon demonstrated.

The first transatlantic communication was sent on 12 December 1901 from Cornwall, England, to Saint John's, Newfoundland, where Marconi had set up receiving equipment.

An 1896 Marconiphone.

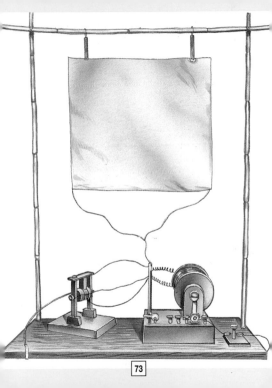

POWERED FLIGHT

The first succesful self-propelled aeroplane was invented by Orville Wright (1871-1948) and Wilbur Wright (1867-1912). The brothers, who formed the Wright Cycle Company in Dayton, Ohio, became interested in aviation in 1896, when they learned of early European attempts at flight, such as those of Otto Lilienthal in Germany, who died that year in a glider accident. They began by carrying out tests with kites and then gliders in order to solve the problems of controlling a plane's motion in flight, inventing ailerons, the movable wingtips that allow a pilot to control his plane. Taking advice from the United States Weather Bureau, the brothers selected an isolated beach near Kitty Hawk, North Carolina, for their flight tests. With more than 700

Orville Wright in the Flyer I.

successful glider flights completed at Kitty Hawk in 1902, the next problem the Wrights faced was finding an engine light enough and powerful enough to get their plane off the ground. Unable to find anyone else willing to take on the job, the brothers designed and built their own 16-horsepower engine and propeller for their plane, Flyer I. On 17 December 1903 Orville achieved the first successful flight ever made in a self-propelled heavier-than-air craft. He stayed in the air for almost a minute and covered 260 metres (850 feet). The newspapers of the time took almost no interest in this momentous event, but within a few years in 1909 Louis Bleriot had completed the first flight across the English Channel and the public imagination was fired by the new invention.

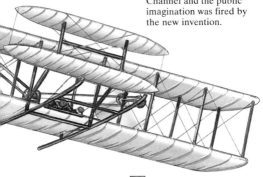

TELEVISION

The invention of the telephone in 1876 led many people to wonder if pictures could be transmitted as well as sound. John Logie Baird (1888–1946) began his experiments with television in 1923. He used a cardboard disk with a spiral of holes that he made out of a hatbox. This was attached to a motor mounted on a tea chest to make it spin. Baird's projection lamp was in a biscuit tin and he used lenses from bicycle lamps to focus the light. A photoelectric cell was placed behind the spinning disc – this generated an electric current that varied according to the brightness of the light reflecting from the object being scanned. The current was transmitted to a neon lamp and the image being scanned was seen by observing the lamp through another spinning disc that matched the first. In 1925 Baird demonstrated his device in Selfridge's department store in London and gained financial backing after the press

covered another demonstration before the Royal Society. He also experimented with sending pictures along telephone lines between London and Glasgow. By 1928 he had developed a colour system and invented a device for storing images on phonograph records. In 1936 he started a regular television service for the BBC but this was scrapped three months later in favour of an electronic system.

Baird's mechanical television.

JET ENGINE

No one inventor can be given all the credit for the invention of jet propulsion. Sir Frank Whittle of Britain, Hans von Ohain and Max Adolf Muller of Germany and Secondo Campini of Italy were all independently involved in the successful development of the turbojet engine. Whittle actually patented a specification for a jet engine in 1930, but it wasn't until 1937 that he succeeded in building his first working engine, the same year that von Ohain and Muller developed their engine in

Germany. Two German research aeroplanes were built by Ernst Heinkel in 1939; the He176 was flown on rocket power some time in June, and the He178 was flown on turbojet power first on 24 August for a short distance and then on 27 August for its first full flight. The first jet fighter was the twin-engined He280, in April 1941, followed later that year by Whittle's Gloster Meteor and Campini's Caproni-Campini CC2. The Gloster Meteor was the first jet to enter service, in July 1944. The German Messerschmitt Me262 was the first jet fighter to engage in aerial combat, in 1945. The first jet transport was the British de Havilland Comet, first flown on 27 July 1949, and entered regular passenger service in May 1952.

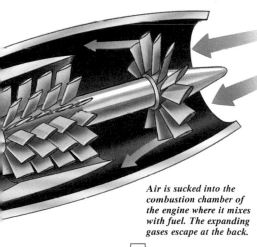

Air is sucked into the combustion chamber of the engine where it mixes with fuel. The expanding gases escape at the back.

THE ROCKET

In 1883, Konstantin Tsiolkovsky, a Russian schoolteacher, produced notebooks containing sketches of spaceships fuelled with liquid oxygen and liquid hydrogen. The occupants were shown in a pressurized cabin with double-wall protection against meteoroids. In 1921, Robert Goddard in the USA began experiments with liquid fuels and on 16 March 1926, at Auburn, Massachusetts, became the first person to launch a liquid-propellant rocket, fuelled by gasoline and liquid oxygen. It reached a height of 12.5 m (41 ft), reached a top speed of 100 km/h (60 mph), and landed 56 m (184 ft) away. In 1927, German rocket enthusiasts founded the Society for Space Travel. They approached the German army and demonstrated their Repulsor rockets. In 1933 a special section of the Army Weapons Department was established. Werner von Braun of the Society for Space Travel was placed in charge of rocket development. In April 1937 a major rocket research station was completed near the village of Peenemunde on the Baltic coast. The large A-4 rocket (called the V2 by the German High Command) was developed here. The V2 was launched against London, Antwerp and other targets in 1944-45. After the war captured V-2s were used for upper-atmosphere research. Von Braun went to the US where he joined the US space programme.

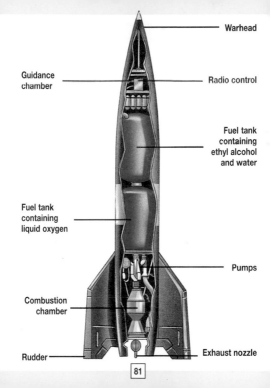

Warhead

Guidance chamber

Radio control

Fuel tank containing ethyl alcohol and water

Fuel tank containing liquid oxygen

Pumps

Combustion chamber

Rudder

Exhaust nozzle

THE ATOMIC BOMB

In 1938, German scientist Otto Hahn succeeded in splitting the uranium atom, leading to the possibility of an atomic chain reaction. Fearing that Nazi Germany might build an atom bomb, scientists convinced President Roosevelt to begin the American effort. The Manhattan Project, as it was called, was spread over 37 sites and

Explosives inside the bomb compress the plutonium to supercritical mass.

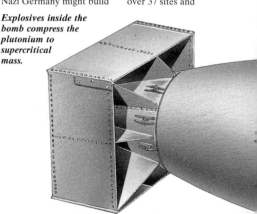

employed 43,000 people. Physicist J. Robert Oppenheimer was appointed director of the weapons laboratory, at Los Alamos, New Mexico. After much difficulty, in 1945 a supply of uranium-235 pure enough to be used in the bomb arrived at Los Alamos, where it was fashioned into a weapon. One piece of uranium was to be fired at another, so that together they formed a supercritical, explosive mass. This bomb was first detonated over the Japanese city of Hiroshima on 6 August 1945. A second type of bomb used plutonium. High explosives were used to compress the plutonium into a supercritical mass. This bomb was tested at Alamogordo, New Mexico, on 16 July 1945, the first atomic bomb to be detonated.

ARTIFICIAL SATELLITE

Any artificial object that orbits an astronomical object in space is called an artificial satellite. The Space Age began on 4 October 1957, when the first artificial satellite, Sputnik 1, was placed in orbit by the Soviet Union. The first American satellite, Explorer, was launched on 31 January 1958.

Today, hundreds of artificial satellites circle the Earth, providing communications links, weather observations, navigational aids, military information gathering and other functions. Most satellites are lifted into orbit by rockets, but the United States has also placed satellites in orbit from the space shuttle. A satellite in Earth orbit is positioned at least 160 km (100 miles) up to avoid its being slowed down by drag on the atmosphere. A satellite that is 35,900 km (22,300 miles) above the Earth's surface will take exactly 24 hours to complete an orbit. If the satellite is positioned over the Equator and is moving in the same direction as the Earth's rotation it will appear to be positioned at a fixed point in the sky. These geostationary orbits, as they are called, are often used for communications satellites. Satellites are usually powered by solar cells with batteries to provide back-up when the satellite is in shadow.

Sputnik 1, the first artificial satellite.

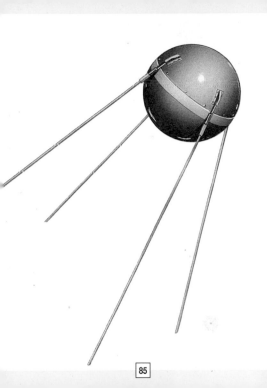

GENETIC ENGINEERING

The cells in your body store a huge amount of information in 100,000 genes located on 46 chromosomes. Together, this information makes up the instructions for making you. Genetic engineering allows scientists to remove specific genes from an organism's chromosomes, to make identical copies of genes, and to take the genetic material from one organism and insert it into a different organism. Genetic engineering was first developed during the late 1960s and early 1970s in experiments with bacteria and viruses. Scientists discovered that bacteria make chemicals called restriction enzymes that cut DNA chains at specific sites. Hamilton O. Smith, discoverer of restriction enzymes, won the Nobel Prize for physiology or medicine in 1978; the first people to use these tools, Daniel Nathans and Werner Arber, shared the prize. Restriction enzymes are the crucial tools of genetic engineering. The DNA molecule is the carrier of genetic information, which is encoded in its structure in the form of compounds called nucleotides.

Restriction enzymes recognize nucleotides arranged in a specific order and cut the DNA in those regions only. Each restriction enzyme recognizes a different sequence of nucleotides, thus allowing scientists to cut chromosomes into different lengths. At least 80 restriction enzymes are now known. Restriction enzymes, used in conjunction with other enzymes that put DNA back together make it possible to produce new combinations of genes that may not exist in nature. At present, genetic engineering only allows a small number of new characteristics to be added to an organism. It is not possible to create a new organism from scratch.

The structure of DNA was determined by James Watson and Francis Crick in 1953.

TIMELINE OF INVENTIONS

c.2,500,000 years ago the first tools are used.

c.1,000,000 years ago people learn to use fire.

c.200,000 years ago stone hand axes are used.

c.25,000 years ago the bow and arrow are invented.

c.5000 BC the first forms of writing appear.

c.4000 BC: the first ploughs are used.

c.3500 BC the wheel is invented.

c.3500 BC: the first sailing ships are built.

c.3000 BC Bronze is used to make tools and weapons.

c.1500 BC The Egyptians invent the sundial.

c.1450 BC The Egyptians invent the water clock or clepsydra.

c.1400 BC Glass is made in Egypt and Mesopotamia.

c.430 BC An optical telegraph, using torches on hilltops, is used in Greece.

c.300 BC A Chinese book contains the first reference to a lodestone.

c.300 BC Cast iron is invented in China.

c.140 BC Paper is made in China and used as a packing material.

c.AD 1 The ship's rudder is invented in China.

105 Ts'ai Lun invents paper that can be used for writing.

400 The umbrella is invented in China.

577 Matches are invented in China.

c.600 The earliest known windmills are built in Persia (Iran).

c.720 Mechanical clocks appear in China.

c.880 Paper money is used in China.

c.1080 Chinese sailors use compasses to navigate at sea.

c.1150 The Chinese make the first rockets.

c.1286 Spectacles are invented.

c.1310 The first mechanical clocks appear in Europe.

c.1450 Johann Gutenberg invents printing with moveable type.

c.1450 Nicholas Krebs makes spectacles to correct near sight.

1502 Peter Henlein makes the first pocket watch.

c.1590 Zacharias Janssen invents the compound microscope.

1608 Hans Lippershey invents the telescope.

1620 Cornelius Drebbel builds the first submarine.

1646 Athanasius Kircher invents the magic lantern.

1654 The Grand Duke of Tuscany invents the sealed liquid thermometer.

1656 Christiaan Huygens develops a pendulum clock.

1679 Denis Papin invents the pressure cooker.

1698 Thomas Savery invents his 'Miner's Friend' the first practical steam-powered machine.

1701 Jethro Tull invents a machine drill for planting seeds.

1712 Thomas Newcomen builds a steam engine using a piston and cylinder.

1742 Anders Celsius invents the Centigrade scale of temperature.

1760 Benjamin Franklin invents the lightning rod.

1765 James Watt redesigns Newcomen's steam engine making it six times as effective.

1769 Joseph Cugnot builds the first steam-driven road vehicle.

1769 Richard Arkwright patents the water-frame spinning machine.

1775 David Bushnell invents a one-man submarine, the Turtle.

1783 Jean François Pilâtre de Rozier and François Laurent, Marquis d'Arlandes, become the first humans to fly, making the first flight in a hot-air balloon designed by the Montgolfier brothers.

1784 Benjamin Franklin invents bifocal glasses.

1792 Claude Chappe invents the optical telegraph.

1792 William Murdoch invents coal-gas lighting.

1800 Alessandro Volta invents the battery.

1804 Nicolas Appert invents canning of food.

1804 Richard Trevithick develops a steam locomotive that runs on rails.

1808 Humphrey Davy develops the first electric-powered lamp, the arc light.

1815 Humphrey Davy invents the safety lamp for use in mines.

1815 John McAdam invents a method of paving roads using crushed rocks.

1816 David Brewster invents the kaleidoscope.

1821 Michael Faraday invents the electric motor.

1822 Charles Babbage develops his Difference Engine, a calculating device.

1822 Joseph Nicéphore Niepce produces the first photograph.

1823 William Sturgeon makes the first electromagnet.

1829 William Austin Burt invents an early version of the typewriter.

1830 Joseph Henry discovers the principle of the dynamo, as does Michael Faraday independently.

1830 Charles Sauria and J.F. Kammerer make matches that light when struck.

1831 Michael Faraday and Joseph Henry, working independently, discover the principle of the electric generator. Henry designs a practical electric motor.

1831 Charles Wheatstone and William Fothergill invent the first electric telegraph.

1832 Charles Babbage invents the first computer, his Analytical Engine. It is never built in working form.

1835 Samuel Colt patents his revolver.

1837 Samuel Morse patents his telegraph using a dot/dash

code he has also invented.

1839 William Talbot invents photographic paper for making negatives.

1845 Robert William Thomson invents the rubber tyre.

1852 Elisha Graves Otis invents the passenger safety elevator.

1859 Gaston Planté invents the rechargeable battery.

1861 James Clerk Maxwell makes the first colour photograph.

1868 Georges Leclanché invents the dry cell battery.

1869 J.F. Tretz invents the bicycle chain.

1876 Alexander Graham Bell patents the telephone.

1876 Karl Paul Gottfried von Linde builds the first practical refrigerator.

1879 Joseph Swan and Thomas Alva Edison produce the first practical electric light bulbs.

1883 Gottlieb Daimler invents the motorboat.

1885 Karl Benz invents the petrol-driven motor car.

1885 Gottlieb Daimler invents the motorbike.

1885 James Dewar invents the thermos flask.

1893 Rudolf Deisel invents the engine that is named after him.

1895 Guglielmo Marconi produces the first practical wireless telegraph system, the forerunner of radio.

1895 Otto Lillienthal builds the first glider that can rise above its take-off height.

1895 Auguste and Louis Lumiere invent the cimematograph.

1901 Hubert Booth invents the vacuum cleaner.

1902 Robert Bosch invents the spark plug.

1903 Wilbur and Orville Wright launch the first succesful aeroplane at Kitty Hawk.

1904 Emile Berliner invents the flat disk phonograph, which is soon adopted by the record industry.

1907 Paul Cornu builds the first helicopter that can carry a human.

1915 Paul Langevin invents sonar.

1917 Clarence Birdseye develops freezing as a method of preserving food.

1925 Vladimir Zworykin patents a colour television system.

1926 The *Jazz Singer*, the first talking motion picture, is released.

1926 The pop-up toaster is invented.

1926 John Logie Baird produces television images.

1926 Robert Goddard launches the first liquid-fuelled rocket.

1928 Joseph Schick invents the electric razor.

1929 FM radio is introduced.

1930 Sliced bread is introduced.

1930 Frank Whittle patents the jet engine.

1932 Television with a cathode-ray picture tube is

demonstrated.

1934 Wallace Hume Carothers invents nylon.

1936 Fluorescent lighting is introduced.

1937 Frank Whittle builds the first working jet engine.

1938 Lazlo Biro invents the ballpoint pen.

1939 The He 178, the first jet-propelled aircraft, is flown.

1943 Jacques-Yves Cousteau invents the Aqualung.

1943 Alan Turing and others develop Colossus, the first electronic calculating device.

1944 The V2 missile become operational.

1945 The first atom bomb is detonated.

1948 Georges deMestral invents Velcro.

1948 Edwin Land invents a camera and film that develops pictures inside the camera.

1948 William Shockley and others invent the transistor.

1954 The first nuclear-powered submarine, *Nautilus*, is commissioned.

1955 Christopher Cockerell develops the first hovercraft.

1957 Sputnik 1, the first artificial satellite, is launched.

1970 The computer floppy disk is introduced.

1971 The microchip is invented.

1971 The electronic pocket calculator is invented.

1982 Compact disk players are introduced.

1983 The computer mouse is introduced.